To my husband - whom I could not have done this without.

To Louisiana Tech University - for fostering an environment that gifted me an unparalleled love for my career field.

And finally, to my mom and dad - the countless hours you spent listening to forestry talk and your unwavering encouragement to never stop pursuing my passions made this all possible.

Copyright © 2026 by Sydney McCoy

All rights reserved. No part of this book may be reproduced or used in any manner without written permission of the copyright owner except for the use of quotations in a book review.

First paperback edition March 2026

Book Illustrations and Design by Jenna Roblee

ISBN 979-8-218-81693-3 (paperback)

Library of Congress Control Number: 2026905264

# T is for Trees:
## The ABCs of Forestry

Written by Sydney Gray

Illustrated by Jenna Roblee

Forestry blends art and science with care,
To manage the forests and protect what's there.

Meeting our goals, both big and small,
While keeping the forests healthy for all.

A is for AXE.

Watch the tree fall.

Axes are great for cutting down one tree at a time.

B is for BURN.

So they can grow tall.

Prescribed burning helps trees grow big and strong by getting rid of nearby plants, so the tree gets all the nutrients in the soil. It also ensures that there is no fuel for possible future wildfires!

# C is for COMPASS.

Which shows you the way.

A compass always points north.

D is for DIBBLE.

To plant trees all day.

Dibble bars are a special type of shovel that helps plant baby trees by hand faster.

# E is for EVERGREEN.
Loved during Christmas time.

Evergreen trees don't lose their leaves in the fall, and they stay green year-round.

F is for **FLAGGING**.
To keep you in line.

Flagging comes in bright colors and is used to show loggers where to stop cutting.

G is for GPS.

To help you find your way.

A GPS has a little blue dot to show where you are and where you're going. It works by talking to satellites in the sky.

H is for HARDHAT.
To keep you safe all day.

A hardhat is made out of a tough material that keeps your head safe, in case anything falls on it. Objects will bounce right off!

# I is for INCREMENT BORER.

To tell you the years.

An increment borer is inserted into a tree and twisted out. It tells you how old the tree is without having to cut it down to count the rings.

J is for J-ROOT.

That causes some tears.

A J-root is the root shape of an incorrectly planted seedling. A J-root causes the tree to grow poorly, as the roots cannot properly reach into the soil.

K is for KNOT.

A big bump on a tree.

A knot on a tree is where a limb used to be but has fallen off.

# L is for LOG TRUCK

They take trees where they should be.

Log trucks hold lots of trees, and deliver them to different mills, depending on the sizes of the trees.

# M is for MILLS.

Where products are made.

Mills turn trees into paper, lumber, boxes—even toothpaste!

# N is for NATURE.

Where trees give us shade.

Nature is home to trees of all sizes. Trees have important jobs, like cooling the earth and producing oxygen so we can breathe.

O is for OPERATOR.

Who drives a machine.

Operators drive all sorts of big machines, like a shear, skidder, and loader.
A shear cuts trees down and a skidder brings those trees to the loader.
The loader puts the trees on a log truck.

# P is for PLANTER.

Who plants trees in a routine.

Planters are workers who specialize in planting trees.
Trees are planted in long rows, just like farm crops such as corn.

Q is for QUERCUS.

Where oak trees will be.

Quercus is the Latin word for oak trees. Oak trees produce acorns.

R is for RINGS.

On the inside of a tree.

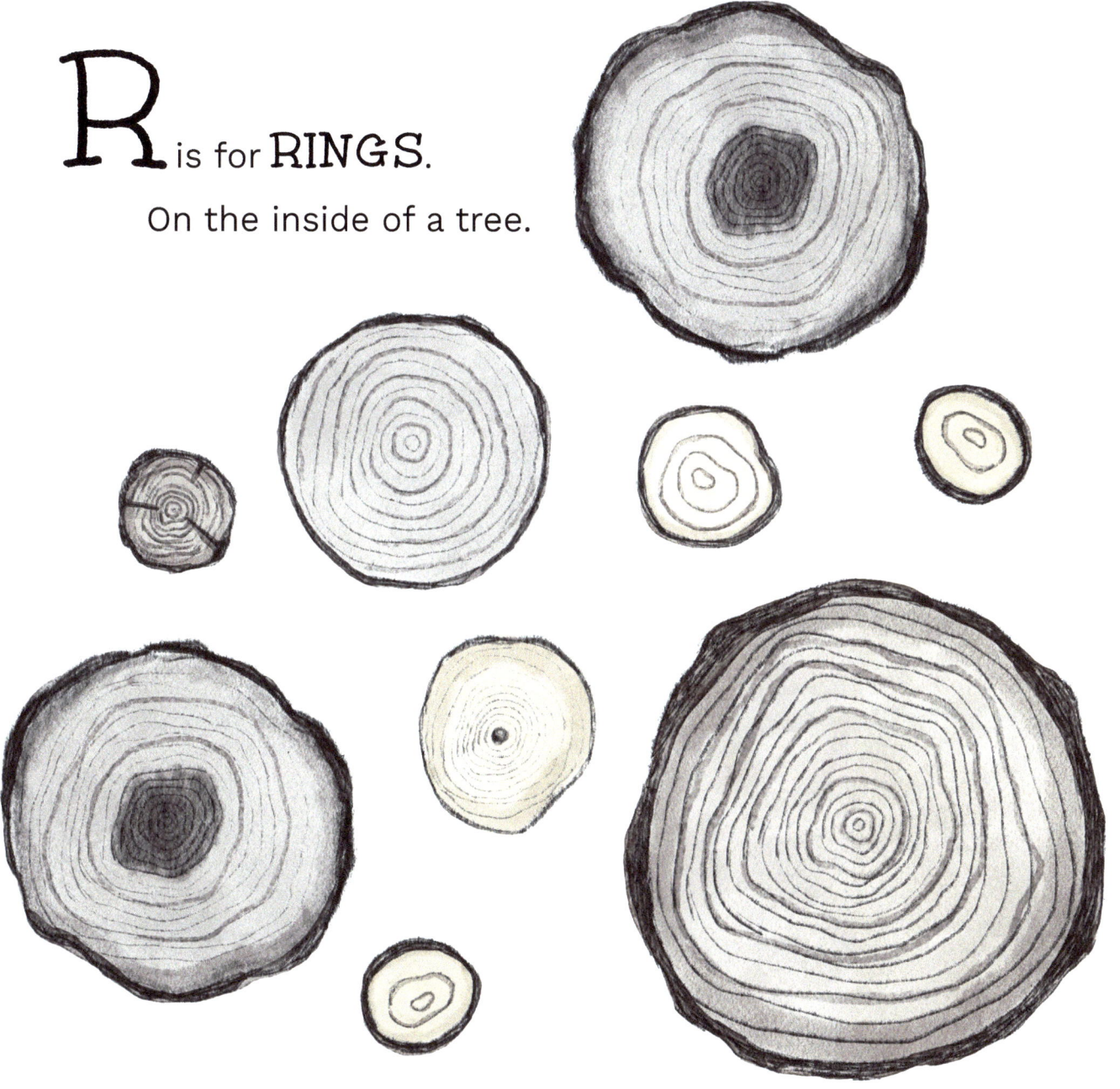

The number of rings a tree has tells you how old it is.

# S is for SEEDLINGS.

Trees that are small and cute.

Seedling is the term for a "baby" tree. A seedling has grown past the seed stage but is not yet a sapling—a young tree.

T is for TREES.

That have many roots.

Roots are channels that bring up water and nutrients from the soil to the tree.

U is for UTV.
One sweet ride.

A UTV is a Utility Terrain Vehicle and it helps get you around fast.

V is for VEST.

To stay safe outside.

A bright-colored safety vest helps others see you in the woods.

# W is for WILDLIFE.

Living in forests like these.

Forests are full of wildlife, including deer, turkeys, rabbits, owls, and doves. Wildlife depends on healthy forests for safe places to sleep and eat.

# X is for XYLEM.

That moves water through trees.

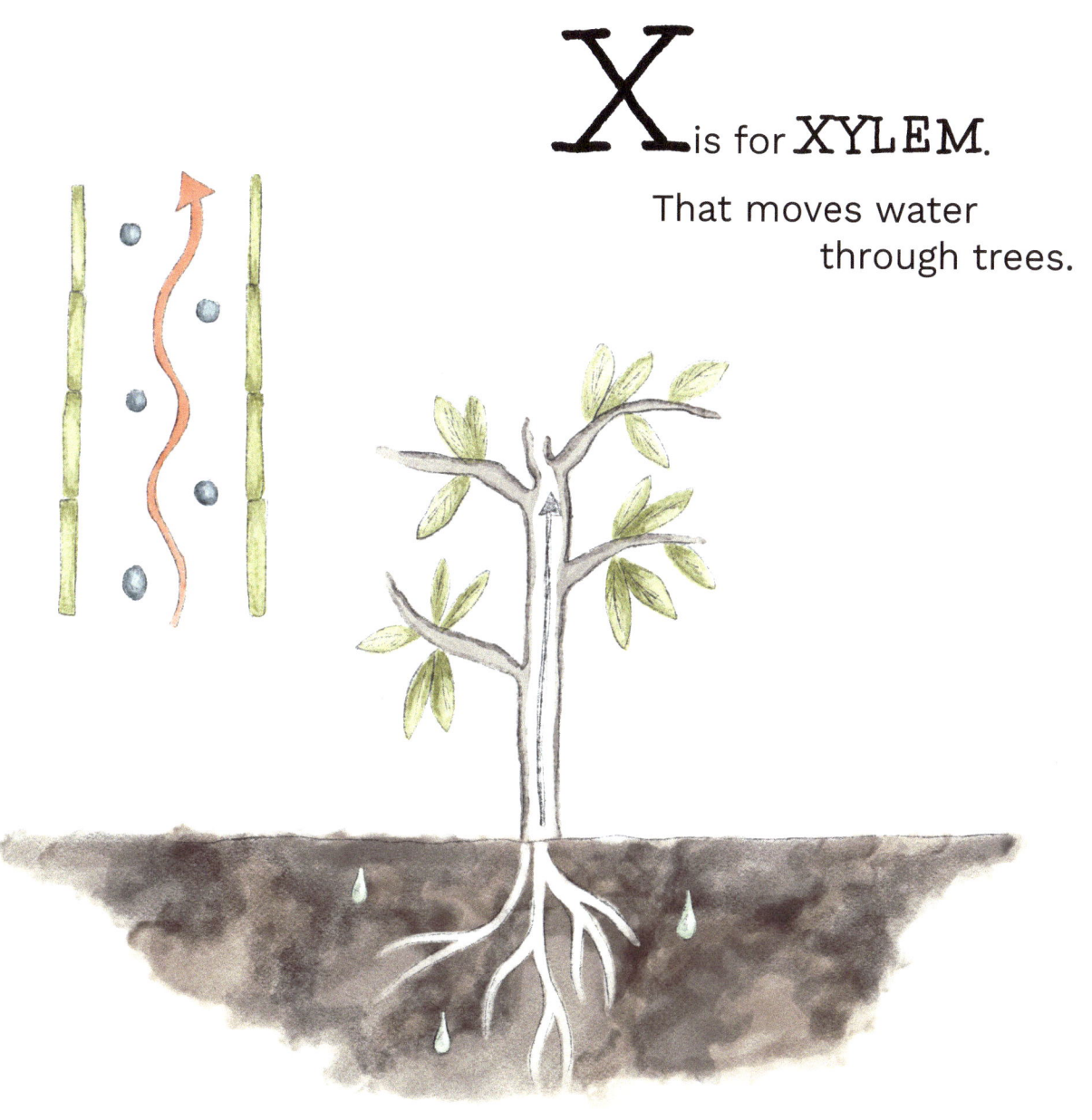

A xylem is like a vein inside a tree, bringing water and nutrients from the tree's roots to the leaves.

# Y is for YARDS.
This one stores logs.

Yards store logs at mills. Wet yards store logs in water.
The water keeps the logs in good condition, like food in your refrigerator!

Z is for ZONE.

Special areas like bogs.

Streamside Management Zones are protected areas of water, like bogs, that keep aquatic animals like fish and frogs safe.

As you can see,
Forestry is a life cycle that helps both you and me.

It helps people one and all,
By making lumber to build houses big and tall.

It gives wildlife homes to thrive
And food sources a space to survive.

When the biggest trees are gone,
New ones are planted to keep growing on.

The cycle starts, it never ends,
Sustaining life for nature's friends.

Sustainable forest management means taking care of forests in a smart way so they stay healthy and productive for a long time. When trees get cut down, they get replanted with new ones to keep the life cycle going. When people manage forests in that careful, sustainable way, the trees grow faster and stronger, animals have more food and better places to live, and we get the wood products that people all over the world need. In this way, both humans and nature can thrive together.

www.ingramcontent.com/pod-product-compliance
Lightning Source LLC
LaVergne TN
LVHW071659060526
838201LV00037B/386